Also by Ferida Wolff and Dolores Kozielski

*The Toothless Vampire
and 99 Other Howl-oween Riddles*

SPITBALLS & SPAGHETTI

OVER 150 LUNCHROOM JOKES & RIDDLES

BY FERIDA WOLFF and
DOLORES KOZIELSKI

ILLUSTRATED BY DARYLL COLLINS

A Trumpet Club Original Book

ISBN 0-590-34153-7

Text copyright © 1995 by Ferida Wolff and Dolores Kozielski.
Illustrations copyright © 1995 by The Trumpet Club.
All rights reserved. Published by Scholastic Inc., 555 Broadway, New York, NY 10012, by arrangement with Scholastic Inc.
TRUMPET and the TRUMPET logo are registered trademarks of Scholastic Inc.

12 11 10 9 8 7 6 5 4 3 2 1   7 8 9/9 0 12/0

Printed in the U.S.A.

For Lauren and Nate
F. W.

For Jim and Bernadette
D. K.

CONTENTS

CONTENTS

WHAT'S FOR LUNCH?

Overheard in the lunch line

ANDY: Mandy, why do you have one eye closed?

MANDY: That way the food only looks half bad.

What happened when two ducks flew in the cafeteria window?
The cook served peanut-butter quackers for lunch.

When are students allowed to have king-sized drinks for lunch?
On reigny days.

Why was it cold in the school cafeteria?
Because they were serving brrr-itos and chili.

How is a swimmer in Athens like a hamburger in the school cafeteria?
They both float in grease.

One day during a terrible storm, the lunchroom lights went out, leaving the cafeteria in darkness.
"I can't see what I'm eating," said Jimmy.
"Me neither," said Timmy, "but it sure tastes better this way!"

What's on the school cafeteria menu today?
Greasy fingerprints.

Why do you get a sinking feeling when you see the Wednesday special?
Because it's submarine sandwiches.

What letters of the alphabet taste great with tomato sauce?
Z T.

What do you have when you leave a sandwich in your lunch box for three days?
A peanut-butter and smelly sandwich.

What kind of eggs do honor students eat?
Grade A.

What's the difference between an entire cookie dipped in a glass of milk and a huge piece of pineapple?
One is a whole dunk and the other is a Dole hunk.

On which day does the school cafeteria sell two tacos for the price of one?
Twosday.

FIRST GRADER (holding tray): This is my first day. Can you tell me a good place to eat?
SECOND GRADER: Yes. At home.

What do you call a big swallow after eating a jalapeño pepper?
The Gulp of Mexico.

What do you tie a lunch box with?
String beans.

Why couldn't the boy stop laughing in the classroom?
He'd just had Snickers for lunch.

Which is better, eating lunch with your fingers or a fork?
It's better to eat lunch with your fingers. A fork doesn't taste good at all.

What's in the middle of the cafeteria?
The letter T.

Why isn't the basketball team allowed to eat in the school cafeteria?
Because they all dribble.

What vegetable should you eat after you eat your peas?
Your Q-cumbers.

What does a cheerleader eat for lunch before a basketball game?
Cheerios.

What sounds just before lunchtime?
The lunch belly.

What's the difference between a steamed wiener and a pig with measles?
One is a hot dog and the other is a dot hog.

Why does Stephanie whistle while she's eating dessert?
Because she has a tweet tooth.

Why is the cafeteria floor painted green?
So everyone can stand on lime.

PETE: Don't you know it isn't cool to bring a thermos to school?
DAN: I hope it's not. I like my soup hot.

JULIE: Joey, can you believe there isn't anything to drink for lunch?
JOEY: Then I guess I'll just have imaginized milk.

FOOD FIGHT

What happened when Jan threw baked spuds on the lunchroom floor?
They became smashed potatoes.

What did the class bully bring to school for lunch?
A knuckle sandwich.

One day Janie went up to the cafeteria cashier and demanded her lunch money back.
"Why? Didn't you like your food?" the cashier asked.
"The spaghetti was fine," said Janie, **"but the spitballs were too soggy!"**

What do an alien invasion and a food fight have in common?
Flying saucers.

Why did the bully punch the can of vegetables?
Because he wanted black-eyed peas.

What do you get when there are lots of kids in the lunch line?
A grilled squeeze sandwich.

FIRST BOY: Hey, quit pushing in line.
SECOND BOY: I just saw what was for lunch, and I'm pushing to get out of line.

DOTTY: Jim, it's a mistake to give that bully your lunch money. You'll be hungry later.

JIM: I know. I'm already paying for my missed steak.

What happened when the school baker ran out of white flour?
He caused a rye-it.

Tongue Twister:
Sally slipped sideways when Sidney spilled soup.

What's red and spicy and is flung around the cafeteria during food fights?
Unidentified flying salsa.

When do most food fights end?
After fling break.

What's enormous, pink, has a curly tail, and scares everyone in the lunchroom?
Pigfoot.

Why does the music teacher eat with the school band in the lunchroom?
To keep them from passing around any notes.

What does the dishwasher do during a food fight?
He throws in the towel.

What does the cafeteria look like after a food fight?
A mush-room.

Why did Mike tell Susan to hit him with an orange and a banana?
Because he wanted some fruit punch.

When does everyone leave the lunch-room?
At dessert time.

What do California and cafeterias have in common?
Plenty of faults.

PRINCIPAL: Julie, I want you to come to my office after you eat your lunch.

JULIE: Okay.

PRINCIPAL (at the end of the day): Julie, why didn't you come to my office after lunch?

JULIE: Because I didn't eat my lunch. I saved it for later.

If some of your friends sit on the left side of the lunchroom and some sit on the right side, where should you sit?

On a chair.

Darla saw two lines in the lunchroom.

"What's the short line for?" she asked Marla.

"To get your food."

"What's the long line for?"

"To go to the nurse's office."

Why was the girl accused of stealing dessert?
Because someone saw her pudding it in her lunch box.

What does the class clown eat for lunch?
Wisecrackers.

Name four things that squeak in the cafeteria.
The door and three mice.

What holds up the menus on the lunch-room bulletin board?
Butterscotch tape.

Why did the boy jump up and down after eating a candy bar and drinking a glass of milk?
He wanted a chocolate milk shake.

What happened when Sybil took Frank's hot dog?
Frank fought her (frankfurter).

LUNCHROOM
HELPERS

RALPH (*holding up two fingers in a V*):
  Peace, man.
SCHOOL COOK: We only have carrots
  today.

CLUCK
CLUCK

Why did the teacher pass the chicken?
Because it knew all the right answers.

TEACHER: Gabby, did you know that there's baking soda in your chocolate chip cookies?
GABBY: No kidding. What kind, cola or root beer?

LUNCHROOM AIDE: Jimmy, what would you like with your sandwich?

JIMMY: The answers to tomorrow's test.

What do the school custodian and a student who gets caught in the rain have in common?

They both have wet mops.

ANDREA: How much does a raisin cost?

COOK: We don't sell single raisins.

ANDREA: You mean I can only buy married raisins?

PRINCIPAL: Can you cook two dozen eggs for the teachers' luncheon on Tuesday?

COOK: No.

PRINCIPAL: Why not?

COOK: Because I only cook eggs on Fry Day.

What kind of TV show does the dish-washer watch between lunch periods?
A soap opera.

CASHIER: Johnny, I thought you said
  you forgot your lunch money.
JOHNNY: I did.
CASHIER: Then how come I saw you give
  Mary a dollar?
JOHNNY: That was my allowance.

What *do* school cooks put on to keep themselves warm?

Plastic wraps.

AIDE: Danny, why are you so hopping mad?

DANNY: Because I found a hare in my soup.

Where does the school cook get all his fresh vegetables?

From the kinder-garden.

Why couldn't the custodian eat his lunch?

Because he forgot his lunch bucket.

What do you call the lunchroom monitor who reports bad behavior?

The snoop of the day.

FOOD SERVER: Do you want a whole-wheat sandwich?

RUSS: No, I want half a wheat sandwich.

HEALTH INSPECTOR: The conditions in this cafeteria are ghastly!

COOK: We don't use gas. Everything's electric.

Bob ran to put his tray on the cart so he could go out to play.

"Don't run in the lunchroom," said the aide.

Bob ran toward the door.

"Hey! I told you not to run in the lunchroom."

"But I'm running out of the lunchroom."

What did the cook get when he planted a poem and a bowl full of chili?
Rhyme-a-beans.

TEACHER: Billy, if I took half this pizza away, how much would be left?

BILLY: None.

TEACHER: Billy, that's wrong. There would be half left.

BILLY: Not when I got done with it.

What did the soccer coach yell when he found out there was roast chicken for lunch?
Fowl!

The cook announced a drawing for three free lunches. To make it fair, she put one stripe on a piece of paper for the turkey lunch, two stripes for the pizza lunch, and three stripes for the fish lunch. Then she had the students reach into a bowl to pick.
"I got the turkey lunch," said Seeta.
"I've got the pizza," said Geeta.
Neeta picked the last one and said, **"It's three stripes and I'm trout."**

What do a teacher who tells students how to eat properly and a train have in common?
They both say "Chew, chew."

Where do math students sit when they eat more than one lunch?
At the two-times table.

When can you take a sandwich from the shelf?
When it's shelf-serve.

What did the honor student say to the cafeteria cashier?
Do you have change for a scholar?

Why did the principal sound the school bell in the cafeteria?
He wanted to give everyone a school ring.

AIDE: Joe, don't chew with your mouth
   open.
JOE: If I don't open my mouth, I can't
   chew.

Where do you put your lunch to keep it
from getting stale?
In your mouth.

What do you call three spoons, two
forks, and five knives?
U-ten-sils.

HOLIDAY SPECIALS

Where do ghosts eat on Halloween?
In the ghoul cafeteria.

Strange things were known to happen on Halloween to anyone who ate the school food. When Bill tried the ravioli special, his hair grew 12 inches.

"I'm not buying lunch anymore," he said. "For all I know, it's hair today, goon tomorrow."

Tongue Twister:
Ada ate eight eggs on Easter eve.

What's on the menu for Groundhog Day?
Hole-some food.

STANLEY: We're having a science test tomorrow. We have to name the four seasons.

MANLEY: That's easy: salt, pepper, mustard, and ketchup.

Valentine's Day Special:
Hearty Beef Stew.

What do you hear in the school cafeteria on April Fools' Day?
Gags and chokes.

In spring, what kind of bird always comes back to roost on the cafeteria windowsill?
The swallow.

What keeps soda cold on Valentine's Day?
Ice cupids.

What do zombies bring for lunch on Halloween?
Chicken plot pies and straw-buries.

Sign on the locked cafeteria door:
Out to Lunch.

What does the class fibber eat for lunch
on April Fools' Day?
A Whopper.

JUSTINE: What's happening in the cafe-
    teria on Columbus Day?
ARTY: They're having a big sail.

TEACHER: Ronnie, who helped you put
    up the Christmas decorations in the
    cafeteria?
RONNIE: I did it all by my elf.

AMANDA: I'm having a big test just after
    Thanksgiving.
COOK: Then you'd better eat turkey
    with cram-berry sauce.

What do kids eat at lunchtime before they sing Christmas carols?
Harmony grits.

What did the cook make for the principal's birthday?
A birthday cod.

When does a monster eat in the school lunchroom?
Any time he wants.

JAMIE: For Presidents' Day, I heard the cook say she's baking a cherry pie to celebrate our forefathers' birthdays.

JACKIE: Four fathers? I only have one father.

LUNCHTIME
READING

I'm Always Hungry
by Ken I. Havemore

What's for Lunch?
by Howie Cooks

Choosing the Right Lunch
by Rita Menyou

How to Eat a Balanced School Lunch
by Carrie A. Tray

Cafeteria Freebies
by Roland Butter

**How to Serve 100 Students
in Less Than an Hour**
by Harry Upnow

Unusual Lunch Recipes
by Henrietta Pigeon

Cleaning the Cafeteria
by Esau Grime

New Lunchroom Recipes
by May B. Good

Improved School Lunches
by Eda Goodmeal

**Don't Lick Your Fingers:
A Book of Lunchroom Manners**
by Barbara Q. Chips

Lunchroom Gossip
by I. Gotta Tell

Cafeteria Rules to Live By
by Dona Dewit

Skipping Lunch
by Betty Starves

Lunchroom Lines
by Hugo Next

The I Love Holidays Handbook
by Val N. Tine

Lunchtime Pals
by Sid Overhere

Is It Lunchtime Yet?
by Isabell Ringing

Easy Lunchtime Recipes
by Cass A. Role

Hot Meals
by Iona Thermos

Make Lunchtime a Happy Time
by Bima Friend

Cafeteria Games
by Hoss N. A. Round

Second Helpings
by Hope I. Getsome

Eating on the Run
by Bea A. Gobbler

School Lunches That Helped Me Become President
by Dwight House

CHOCK-FULL OF KNOCK-KNOCKS

Knock, knock.
Who's there?
Super.
Super who?
Super salad with your sandwich?

Knock, knock.
Who's there?
Amy.
Amy who?
Amy that spitball at me and I'll amy one at you.

Knock, knock.
Who's there?
Wilma.
Wilma who?
Wilma lunch be ready soon?

Knock, knock.
Who's there?
Udell.
Udell who?
Udell the teacher I threw food in the lunchroom, and you're in big trouble.

Knock, knock.
Who's there?
Artichokes.
Artichokes who?
Artichokes whenever they serve sloppy joes for lunch.

Knock, knock.
Who's there?
Luke.
Luke who?
Luke at what they're serving for lunch today!

Knock, knock.
Who's there?
Samuel.
Samuel who?
Samuel be in charge of cleaning up after lunch.

Knock, knock.
Who's there?
Sid.
Sid who?
Sid down and eat your lunch.

Knock, knock.
Who's there?
Candace.
Candace who?
Candace be all we're having for lunch?

Knock, knock.
Who's there?
Caesar!
Caesar who?
Caesar! She's running away with my fruit cup.

Knock, knock.
Who's there?
Defeat.
Defeat who?
Defeat must not be placed on de table in de school cafeteria.

Knock, knock.
Who's there?
Michael.
Michael who?
Michael be late for lunch if he doesn't hurry.

Knock, knock.
Who's there?
Plato.
Plato who?
Plato potatoes for St. Patrick's Day.

Knock, knock.
Who's there?
Ben.
Ben who?
Ben to lots of schools, but this one has the worst food!

Knock, knock.
Who's there?
Carla.
Carla who?
Carla doctor. I think I've been poisoned!

Knock, knock.
Who's there?
Stan.
Stan who?
Stan in line for me. I'll be right back.

Knock, knock.
Who's there?
Zenda.
Zenda who?
Zenda note to the cook—this food is awful!

Knock, knock.
Who's there?
Disguise.
Disguise who?
Disguise always pushing in the lunch line.

MIXED-UP
MEANINGS

A sunburned scaredy-cat:
Fried chicken

Strawberry shortcake:
A dessert without many strawberries

Currant event:
A raisin fight in the school cafeteria

Cold cuts:
Iced boo-boos

Brown cow:
A chocolate milk container

A broken lunch bell:
A lemon peal

The cook's borrowed mixer:
A lender blender

A cook from another school checking out the fruit dessert:
Apple spy

An overfed nerd:
A stuffed turkey

An earthquake that shook the oven during baking:
A cookie jar

A hot vegetable game played in Idaho:
Mr. Baked Potato Head

A whale with a large vocabulary:
Moby Dictionary